HARRY CALLAHAN

MULTIPLE EXPOSURE 1965

HARRY CALLAHAN

With an introductory essay by Sherman Paul

THE MUSEUM OF MODERN ART, NEW YORK

Preface

Harry Callahan has loved photography with an intensity and constancy that suggest the example of Alfred Stieglitz, who called photography his passion. For twenty-five years he has demonstrated that the most accessible of subjects, approached with the most transparent of techniques, can be made new again each day by precision of feeling.

Callahan's work was first shown at The Museum of Modern Art in 1948, and has since been exhibited in fourteen temporary exhibitions here, most fully in 1962 in a two-man show with Robert Frank. The Museum is pleased to be able now to publish this survey of Callahan's photography—to make it available as broadly as possible to the thousands who have been and will be his students, either in person or through the example of his work.

For their contributions to this book, special thanks are due to Sherman Paul, not only for his illuminating essay, but for his valued suggestions concerning editing and organization of the pictures; to Grace Mayer for the chronology, to Bernard Karpel for the bibliography, and to Dee Knapp for her assistance in preparing both documents; and not least to Harry Callahan, for his counsel and gracious cooperation in all stages of the book's preparation.

John Szarkowski
DIRECTOR, DEPARTMENT OF PHOTOGRAPHY

Contents

THE PHOTOGRAPHY OF HARRY CALLAHAN BY SHERMAN PAUL 6

ELEANOR 11

THE CITY 29

LANDSCAPE 57

CHRONOLOGY BY GRACE M. MAYER 76

SELECTED BIBLIOGRAPHY PREPARED BY BERNARD KARPEL 80

The Photography of Harry Callahan

When looking at the photographs of Harry Callahan one must replace a first impression, accurate enough, of the narrowness of their visual world with an impression, steadily deepened by further study, of a genuine world of vision. To have a camera – it is a memorable experience of childhood – is to be suddenly excited by the wealth of things to see, and by seeing them. Yet with all the world before him Callahan has searched out only his things – the things that express, he has said, "my feelings and visual relationships to the life within me and about me." He does not use the camera as a visual instrument that teaches us to see without its aid; that is the profound socio-aesthetic intent of the documentary art of a Dorothea Lange. He prefers to use it to see the things of the self, for the things he sees are images of the self-and-world. "I am interested," he wrote in an early statement of purpose, "in relating the problems that affect me, to some set of values that I am trying to discover and establish as being my life. I want to discover and establish them through photography."

This proposal, he acknowledged, was a "lifetime project" that required him to employ photography as a means of awareness, of contact with his environment. Having begun as a hobbyist, he had learned in a brief course with Ansel Adams that photography is an art – and a vocation – and he had determined to make it his way of life. His proposal, submitted for a fellowship in 1946 to The Museum of Modern Art, did not present anything more definite than a way of going about living that Callahan had already tried out in the intervals from work that he afforded himself. He wished "to regulate a pleasant form of living, to get up in the morning – free to feel the trees, the grass, the water, sky or buildings or people – everything that affects us; and to photograph that which I saw and have always felt." He was compelled, like Thoreau, to undertake a self-exploratory adventure on life; and so he managed, when not at work teaching photography at the Institute of Design of the Illinois Institute of Technology (1946–1961) or at the Rhode Island School of Design, to take daily excursions in his immediate surroundings, to engage in the act of seeing, and to bring back images of experience for his file – his journal – from which the materials of his exhibitions and books have been selected.

His artistic growth and the course of training he pursued are suggested by the program in photography that he developed, with Arthur Siegel and Aaron Siskind, at the Institute of Design during the directorship of László Moholy-Nagy. The general aim was "to open an individual way," to proceed from "the abstract, the impersonal, the exploratory to the personally expressive." Training was primarily in awareness: to tone, texture, light; to the "basic forms" of natural objects and the "meaning" of things. Though technically sophisticated – multiple exposure and solarization, for example, were taught – such training put every skill at the service of "expressive ends."

In this assimilation of advanced technique to subjectivity, in this concern for the education of artists, one recognizes the auspices of the New Vision, which brought back to Chicago its greatest heritage: the pragmatic-organic tradition of John Dewey and Louis Sullivan. Harry Callahan is a Chicago photographer; and the photography section of the Institute of Design, where he was "master," is the most recent "Chicago School." Significantly, some of his students, under the direction of Aaron Siskind, have engaged for several years in a complete photographic study of the architecture of Adler and Sullivan, and are among the most ardent proponents of Sullivan's art and thought. More profoundly, in the polarities of masculine and feminine, of city and nature, so evident in his work, and in his desire to restore the claims of feeling and selfhood, Callahan shares much with Sullivan.

Callahan speaks of his way of working as "photographing intuitively." He has never been satisfied with the "literal value" of things and has tried to reveal "the subject in a new way to intensify it." He does not, to borrow Thoreau's words, "underrate the value of a fact" – he respects reality and never distorts it – for he knows that attended to "it will one day flower in a truth." Such truths are what Thoreau meant by "correspondences" and Stieglitz by "equivalents": images of inner reality – outer reality seen into and disposed on the plane of imagination. "We must look a long time," Thoreau said, "before we can see." But when we do, the things of this world become ours and constitute a world of vision.

It is apparent in the groups and series into which Callahan's work readily falls that he has looked long enough and discovered certain obsessional images and themes. Large exhibitions of his work, at the Art Institute of Chicago in 1951 and at George Eastman House in 1958, were arranged in this way, though in the former, experiment with technique rather than the thematic significance of subject matter, which Callahan considers most important, seemed determinative. *Photographs: Harry Callahan*, the fullest display in book form, published in 1964 by the El Mochuelo Gallery, takes advantage of the inherent thematic drama of these series and groups – the drama of pursuing an image, which to some extent becomes an image incrementally, and the drama of juxtaposing their groupings. Callahan himself arranged the photographs in this monograph in five groups, but the thematic significance of his work is more forcibly grasped when it is placed in three groups, under the following headings: Eleanor, the City, Landscape.

Any presentation of Callahan's work must begin with studies of his wife Eleanor, the primary inspiration of his art. Emerging mysteriously from the water, Eleanor dominates his world. She is the center of the landscape: the woman among the trees, on the dunes, at rest in the sumac glade; the looming statue in the park, herself a natural fact. Similarly, she is the center of the domestic world, an object of infinite delight, showing up the geometrical emptiness, the flat bare planes, with the volume, curve, and texture of her body. For Callahan, as for William Carlos Williams – who admired his work and whose poetry often provides parallels to it – "There is / no good in the world except out of / a woman. . . ." Callahan's reclining nudes are especially famous, but in the absence of other photographs of Eleanor one could not tell the intensity of his devotion to the eternal feminine.

In his nudes is felt the special stillness that invests his world. His cityscapes possess, as David Ebin has noted, a "weird quietude"; his landscapes, which are often little carpets of ground, are still with the "more pregnant motion" of stillness that William Carlos Williams observed in the rhythmic accompaniment of raindrops on a cat-briar. Nothing is more wonderfully quiet than Callahan's trees, those stately presences abiding winter. His nudes have this stillness and serenity, virtues, however, belonging as much to the artist as to the object, measures of his devotion and what Peter Pollack has called "a still kind of reticence." Toward them, as toward the natural landscape that is feminine (the superimposition of the female body on it insists on this immemorial identification), his attitude is reverential. For he respects sex, in the distinction of Henry Adams, as force rather than as sentiment. In the creases of a woman's buttocks he has depicted a cross. And he has also superbly rendered his veneration in a photograph, difficult at first to apprehend, of the mound of a woman's pregnant belly.

Here, the landscape is the human body, and the mound, bearing light out of the surrounding darkness, is primordial creation. Callahan's world begins and ends here. The stone-textured primitive shape is his temple of life.

From this private intimate world where the eye caresses the object, Callahan turns to an anonymous public world, abandoned, vacuous, almost devoid of life. The study of the lines of the highway (page 31) and the abstraction *Detroit 1945* (page 30) are interesting for their composition, not their human content. The details of signboards and peeling walls that he has photographed may, as in the work of Aaron Siskind, remind one of the paintings of abstract expressionists, but in this context render the visible detritus of culture. Somehow these signs are connected with the forsaken nineteenth-century buildings whose façades Callahan so closely inspects. In these photographs, the lack of foreground, with the suggestion of a continuous plane, an endless wall, is depressing; and the visual precision, an evidence of Callahan's care for these objects, intensifies their vacuity. Not only are these façades (so clearly faces, and perhaps female faces, as Minor White suggests) depthless, but filling the frame makes them heavy and portentous. The brilliant compositional detail of *Chicago 1949* (page 36) – the keystones, fire escape, wire fence, clump of bushes – does not cancel the dark curves of the expressionless windows; and the bright lighting of *Wells Street, Chicago 1949* (page 32) does not reduce the sense of dereliction. They are such façades with "blank and staring eyes" as Williams described in *Paterson I*. Only in one photograph does a light from within beckon and remind one of an interior life—of the domestic function of most of these old buildings.

There is a picture of Eleanor and Barbara that may be considered here by way of transition to the studies of "downtown," the metropolitan heart. Mother and child stand in the very center of an inhospitable industrial-urban space, a de Chirico scene, but convey an indomitable content that nullifies the surroundings. This is the only picture in which the hard textures and unlimited planes, the inexpressiveness and monumental scale of the man-made world do not oppress its denizens.

For the pictures of the city are joyless, punishing. Though Callahan places and dates them, cities are cities, all alike, timeless, infernal. The cities in which he has worked – Chicago, New York, Providence, Asheville, Aix-en-Provence – are places of darkness, gigantic canyons into which a little light seeps down. Most often they seem empty, the few passers-by or a jaywalker representing a common urban phenomenon, the lonely crowd. Except for a recent photograph in which the skyscrapers lean crazily, one never looks upward; one isn't made to, because the city, as Callahan sees it, no longer soars. None of his cityscapes has the dramatic vital quality that rejoices one in Stieglitz's photographs of the metropolitan milieu: no tower climbs into the sun, no tree blossoms from the glistening sidewalk. The weather does not visit this place; there are none of the riches that make a city – wharves and ships, railroad yards, great bridges, the thick life. The city has become "downtown," mostly a place of women, though not feminine, where shoppers painfully come and go, heedless of each other, "walking," as Williams observed in *Paterson*, "indifferent through / each other's privacy." A remarkable multiple exposure (page 34) fixes this experience for us (we at least attend). Other photographs comment on it: one, perhaps humorously, directs us to the cigar of a callous aggressive man walking in the company of an attractive woman (page 47); another, taken in Asheville, shows a woman passing unaware of the single watchful eye of an oculist's sign; and still another, with stunning art, dramatizes a terrifying indifference: in the corridor between a fence and a cold wall, a man with a darkly lit rigid face is about to pass a girl whose face is awkwardly upturned to the light; the design compels an intersection or meeting, but the light bulb will never flash recognition (page 41).

Within this group another series, entitled *Chicago*, presents faces close-up, never in their entirety but always filling the field. In one photograph, a woman is talking eagerly into the ear of another. The other photographs are of a heavily made-up tarnished matron, a young direct-looking Negress, a delicate young woman in profile, a young blonde with Clara Bow rouged lips and heavy earrings (who, like all the others, has "had it"), two women pained by the light, and a face, presumably of a woman but indeterminate, which suggests the sexual affliction that is perhaps one source of the weariness common to most of them. Faces, not bodies – these are the register of the city – and their textures are an aspect of acute characterization, as are the pieces of jewelry, usually earrings, that Callahan frequently manages to include.

The poverty of Callahan's city is spiritual. The people in these cityscapes are in motion, never at rest. Like the well-dressed, constrained woman walking alone on the vast sidewalk against a black background, they seem to be coming out of nowhere and going into nothing. Where one feels the impenetrable facelessness of the façades, here one feels the void. Even the circus, visually exploited by multiple exposure, yields no exuberance. The city is neither exciting nor sinister, just a commonplace perdition, like the Unreal City of Eliot's *The Waste Land*, where the narrator, observing similar people, tells us that "I had not thought death had undone so many."

The lack of real drama in the lives of these people creates the dramatic value of these photographs, which tell us that the city is no longer the great stage of life. A multiple exposure like *Alley, Chicago 1948* (page 34) conveys, in the play of vertical lines and lighted horizontal planes with people moving on them, some sense of the vitality and intensity of a city; and in the multiple exposure where the city seems to pursue the bathers to the water's edge, there is an intimation of natural restoration. But the beneficence of life is not fully redeemed until the final group of photographs, the studies of nature that complement those of Eleanor and enclose the brutally masculine with the sustaining feminine.

These photographs are among the best work by Callahan. They are neither picturesque nor sentimental, do not permit distraction but compel close attention to the natural object; and this concern for the object, as in the similar art of Williams' nature poems, awakens a perception of its intrinsic perfection. Callahan values especially the delicacy of natural things, evoked, for example, in *Royal Oak, Michigan 1945* (page 61) by the imposition of the darker on the lighter image; their refinement, whether of line, pattern, or texture; and their gracefulness, their rhythmic motion of "expressiveness," as in *Cattails against Sky* (page 63). The photograph of spear-like reeds made vibrant by faint ripples of reflection is, like many other studies, oriental in the "refinements of vision" that for Hugo Weber recall the art of Hokusai. Studies of the delicate play of sunlight on water (page 58) also suggest the white writing of Mark Tobey, others the fine draughtsmanship of Klee; and *Multiple-Exposure Tree* (page 66) pulsates with the universal energy, like a nightscape by van Gogh.

Nothing vast or titanic compromises Callahan's confidence in nature, represented best, perhaps, by his winter trees, which, like Williams', are "wise" and "stand sleeping in the cold." In his fields of leaves and grasses one finds only "the pleasing friendships and unanimities of nature" that reminded Thoreau that "a wise purveyor" had been there before him. Callahan's woods, though usually dark, have small inviting recesses and are never threatening; there one would be sure to discover a field of ferns in pewterish splendor. And where nature is so domestic, one may move freely again in nakedness, like the playfully human weed-stalk in its dance of life (page 68).

This world of vision is secured by mastery of technique. Among the triumphs of Callahan's exploration of his imagery are two superimpositions: one of the thighs and mons Veneris (page 20) on a flowering landscape (was it the French landscape that released him?); the other, a recent photograph of the frowning face of a woman, perhaps Eleanor, on a cityscape of shoppers. Superimposition, here, serves the purpose of metaphor (of those complex "images" that Ezra Pound has said are the result of placing "one idea . . . on top of another"); as with multiple images, which Callahan has used to create the illusion of motion and to dislocate images in a cubist fashion, it is a way of employing and asserting the imagination. He is entirely modernist in his art work – Ebin says that he is "abstract, experimental, subjective," and Pollack has pointed out the cubist lack of depth in some of his work (see especially Callahan's book, *The Multiple Image*, 1961) and his concern with photograph as photograph, as created object. But he is not abstract in a technical sense – by abstracting he enables us to see the object – and he is not experimental in perverse and meaningless ways. Williams, as much a romantic formalist as Callahan, understood Callahan's achievement, when, on looking at his photographs in Larry Eigner's book of poems, *On My Eyes*, he associated their beautiful clarity with the art of Pieter Brueghel. For Brueghel fulfilled the requirements of art:

> *Pieter Brueghel the artist saw it [the Nativity]*
> *from the two sides: the*
> *imagination must be served –*
> *and he served*
> > *dispassionately*

Callahan succeeds because he serves the imagination while never relinquishing the values for art contained in the permanent language of man. He revivifies our values by making us aware of them and of what threatens them. His art belongs with the body of major work in our time that seeks to redress the frightening masculinity of our culture. In his work we again discover the intimate spaces of life.

ELEANOR

ELEANOR 1951

ELEANOR 1948

ELEANOR 1948

LEFT: ELEANOR, INDIANA 1948

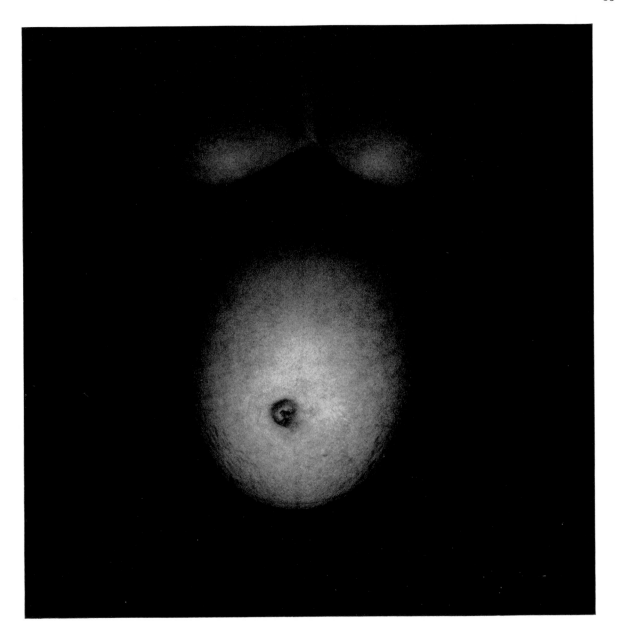

ELEANOR 1949

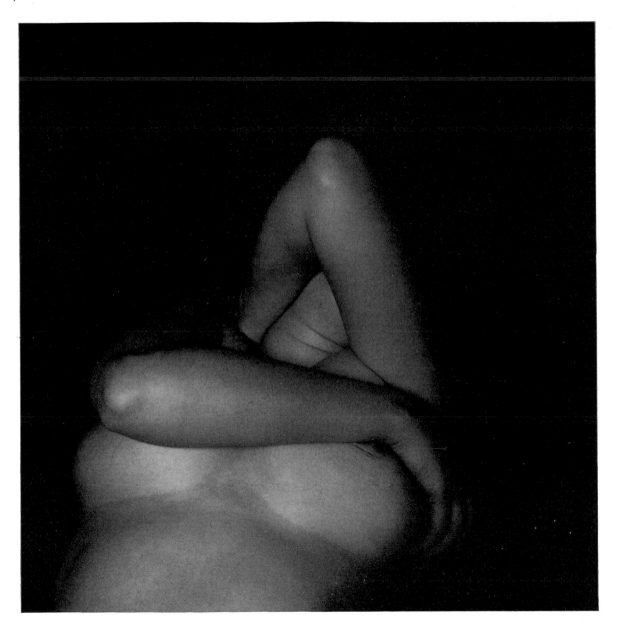

ELEANOR, CHICAGO 1948

ELEANOR 1953

LEFT: ELEANOR, CHICAGO 1949

LEFT: AIX-EN-PROVENCE 1958

ELEANOR, PORT HURON 1954

ELEANOR, CHICAGO 1956

ELEANOR AND BARBARA, CHICAGO 1954

CHICAGO 1956

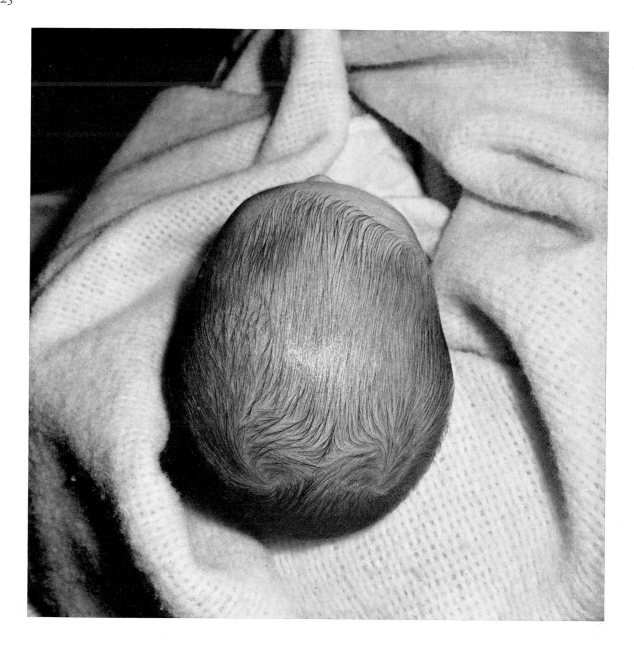

CHICAGO 1950

CHICAGO 1950

ELEANOR AND BARBARA, CHICAGO 1953

THE CITY

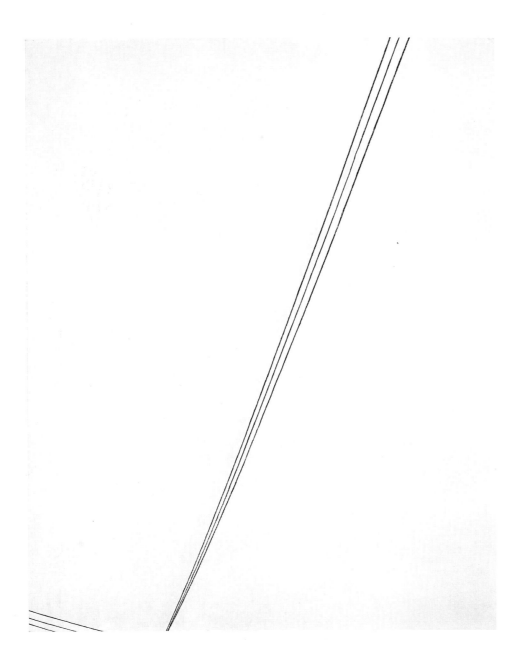

DETROIT 1945

CHICAGO ca. 1949

WELLS STREET, CHICAGO 1949

CHICAGO 1949

ALLEY, CHICAGO 1948

CIRCUS, CHICAGO 1955

CHICAGO 1949

CHICAGO 1950

CHICAGO 1950

RANDOLPH STREET, CHICAGO 1956

CHICAGO 1960

WABASH AVENUE, CHICAGO 1958

CHICAGO 1959

CHICAGO 1961

NEW YORK 1962

PROVIDENCE 1965

LEFT: CHICAGO 1961

PROVIDENCE 1966

49

PROVIDENCE 1967

NEW YORK 1965–1966

RIGHT: SKYSCRAPER, CHICAGO 1953

HIGHLAND PARK, MICHIGAN 1941

LEFT: CHICAGO 1954

CHICAGO 1953

MIDWEST ca. 1949

LANDSCAPE

DETROIT 1941

DETROIT 1942

GRASSES IN SNOW, DETROIT 1943

RIGHT: ROYAL OAK, MICHIGAN 1945

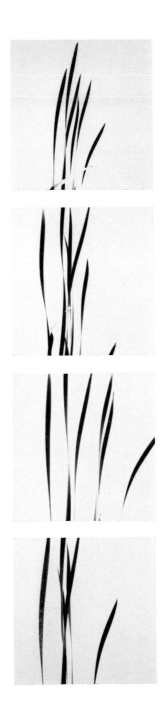

CATTAILS AGAINST SKY 1948

LEFT: MICHIGAN 1948

LAKE MICHIGAN 1949

AIX-EN-PROVENCE 1957

LEFT: MULTIPLE EXPOSURE TREE, CHICAGO 1956

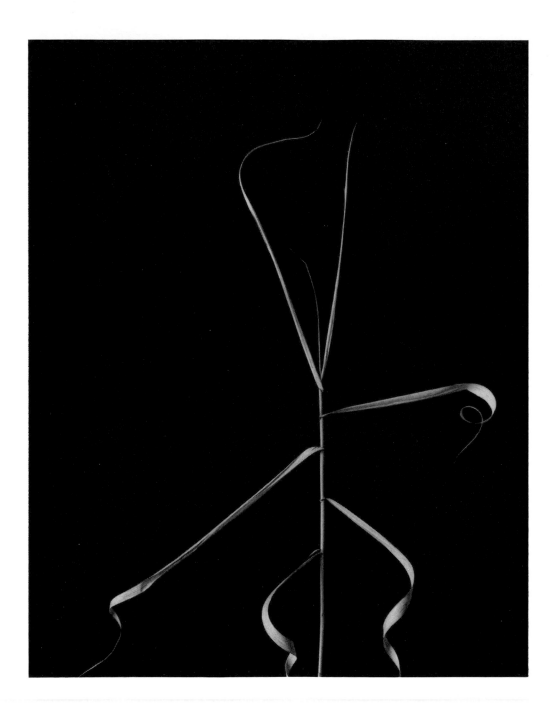

GRASSES, WISCONSIN 1959

LEFT: AIX-EN-PROVENCE 1958

NEW HAMPSHIRE 1961

RHODE ISLAND 1965–1966

RHODE ISLAND 1965

RIGHT: CAPE COD 1964

PROVIDENCE 1967

PROVIDENCE 1967

Chronology by Grace M. Mayer

1912
October 22: Born in Detroit, Michigan, the only son of Harry Arthur Callahan (died in 1957) and Hazel Mills Callahan (living in Port Huron, Michigan); two sisters, Alice C. McKinnon and Mrs. John T. Gauss.

EARLY 1930S
After attending school in Royal Oak, Michigan, and studying engineering for a time at Michigan State College, went to work for the Chrysler Motor Parts Corporation.

1936
November 25: Married Eleanor Knapp, who was to become the subject of many of his most meaningful photographs; their daughter Barbara (born February 6, 1950) has similarly served as inspiration.

1938
First became engrossed in photography as a hobbyist, through a family friend who owned a movie camera. Soon afterward turned to still photography in the company of Todd Webb, with whom he is still in close rapport.

1941
Only education in photography consisted of sporadic attendance at lectures, while a member of the Detroit Photo Guild; the photographs of Ansel Adams, seen at two weekend sessions at the Guild, were the first to affect him strongly; other influences were the photography and philosophy of Alfred Stieglitz.

1944–1945
Worked as a processor in the photo lab of General Motors Corporation.

1945
Lived in New York City for six months, giving himself what he called "a personal fellowship."

1946
Invited by Arthur Siegel, then Head of the Photography Department at Chicago's Institute of Design (a continuation of the Bauhaus, in 1950 to become part of the Illinois Institute of Technology) to join the staff there; a meeting with László Moholy-Nagy resulted in his appointment as an instructor; he was to reside in Chicago for the next fifteen years.

1948
One of the most meaningful relationships of his life— a twenty-year friendship with Edward Steichen (Director of the Department of Photography at The Museum of Modern Art, New York, 1947–1962) was initiated through the inclusion of his photographs in the Museum exhibitions *In and Out of Focus* (April 6– July 11) and *50 Photographs by 50 Photographers* (July 27–September 26). Met Aaron Siskind, who at the opening of his own 1965 retrospective at George Eastman House paid tribute: "Homage to my friend, Harry Callahan. . . . His restlessness has driven him to extend the expressive image of photography."

1949–1950
Placed in charge of the Department of Photography at the Institute of Design of the Illinois Institute of Technology. December 1–January 30, 1950: 13 prints in exhibition *Four Photographers* (with Lisette Model, Bill Brandt, and Ted Croner), The Museum of Modern Art.

1950
April 30–June 4: in exhibition *Photography at Mid Century*, Los Angeles County Museum of Art. August 2–September 17: in *51 American Photographers: New Purchases*, The Museum of Modern Art.

1951
April 23–May 31: one-man show (about 50 prints), The Art Institute of Chicago. April: in Photokina:

Internationale Photo - und - Kino - Ausstellung, Cologne, receiving a diploma and plaque in recognition of his contribution. May 2–July 4: 18 prints in exhibition *Abstraction in Photography*, The Museum of Modern Art. July 13–August 12: in *Twelve Photographers*, The Museum of Modern Art. Summer: taught at the Bauhaus-oriented Black Mountain College, North Carolina, with Aaron Siskind, whom he invited to join him on the faculty of the Illinois Institute of Design; also had exhibition at the College. September 1951–April 1958: one-man circulating exhibition (15 prints) in series "Leading Photographers" sent on tour by The Museum of Modern Art.

1952
May 21–September 1: in Edward Steichen's exhibition *Diogenes with a Camera I* (58 prints), The Museum of Modern Art.

1953
May 15–July 1: in exhibition *Photographs Purchased from Peabody Fund Donation*, The Art Institute of Chicago. August 29–October 4: in exhibition of contemporary photography at the National Museum of Modern Art, Tokyo (American participation arranged by Edward Steichen and Porter McCray).

1954
November 27–January 27, 1955: in Prof. Dr. Otto Steinert's *Subjektive Fotografie 2*, State School of Arts and Crafts, Saarbrücken.

1955
January 24–May 8: in exhibition (and book) *The Family of Man*, created by Edward Steichen for The Museum of Modern Art, and then circulated throughout the world.

1956
January 3–19: one-man show (142 photographs), Kansas City Art Institute. January: in exhibition *Crea-tive Photography—1956*, Lexington Camera Club and University of Kentucky. Alain Jouffroy, reviewing the XXVIII Biennale, Venice (see bibl. 47), comments on the *American Artists Paint the City* exhibition in the United States Pavilion: "But perhaps the work in which the city is best expressed is the large photomontage exhibition at the entrance of the pavilion, a photograph by Harry Callahan." July 15–September 1: in exhibition *Photographs from the Peabody Collection of The Art Institute of Chicago*. November 11–December 21: in exhibition *5 Photographers* (with DeCarava, Hyde, Levinstein, Obsatz), A Photographer's Gallery, New York. December 16–January 13, 1957: in exhibition *Creative Art Photography*, Montclair Art Museum, Montclair, New Jersey. Only photographer to receive Graham Foundation award for Advanced Studies in the Fine Arts, a $10,000 stipend hailed by *Time* (December 31, 1956) as the "highest grant ever given to a photographer."

1957
Uses fellowship to take a year's leave of absence (extending into 1958) in Europe to pursue his own photography, living with his family in Aix-en-Provence. November 14–December 11: in exhibition *Harry Callahan—Aaron Siskind: Photographes Américains*, Centre Culturel Américain, Paris. 1957–1958: in The American Federation of Arts circulating exhibition *Abstract Photography: Aaron Siskind, Harry Callahan, Arthur Siegel, Arthur Sinsabaugh*.

1958
January 10–March 10: one-man exhibition (a retrospective of over 300 prints) is held at George Eastman House, eliciting the following in a review by Minor White (*Aperture*, Number 6:2, 1958, p. 73): "It seems that the decade of photographs in the exhibit . . . contains a phase of Callahan's work as fully as a basket holds a loaf of bread. And I think that I see premoni-

tions of a new facet of the man facing the public. November 26–January 18, 1959: in exhibition *Photographs from the Museum Collection*, The Museum of Modern Art.

1959

April 2–24: in exhibition *Photographer's Choice, Number 1*, Department of Art, Indiana University, Bloomington. September 18–November 8: in exhibition *Masterpieces of Photography from the Museum Collection*, The Art Institute of Chicago. November–December: in exhibition *Photography at Mid-Century*, George Eastman House.

1960

February 16–April 10: 17 prints in exhibition *The Sense of Abstraction in Contemporary Photography*, The Museum of Modern Art. October 1–16: in sales exhibition *Photographs for Collectors*, sponsored by the Junior Council of The Museum of Modern Art, a project in which he becomes a best seller.

1961

January 14–February 7: in exhibition *Director's Choice*, Philadelphia Museum College of Art. February 27–April 2: in exhibition *Six Photographers* (10 prints), College of Fine and Applied Arts, University of Illinois, Urbana. Summer: one-man show at Superior Street Gallery, Chicago, reviewed by F. Franz Schulze in *Art News* (Summer, 1961, p. 67) as the "superb work of Harry Callahan, one of the few photographers in America who can meet the challenge of a gallery environment." October–January 1, 1962: in exhibition *Twentieth Century American Art*, at Kalamazoo Institute of Arts. Resigned from the Illinois Institute of Technology to head the Department of Photography at the Rhode Island School of Design, Providence, as associate professor; here he developed a major in photography and a master's program in photography; moved to Providence, where he bought a home in 1964.

1962

January 29–April 1: 123 prints in exhibition *Photographs by Harry Callahan and Robert Frank*, The Museum of Modern Art. July 28–August 6: in Eighth World Festival of Youth and Students for Peace and Friendship, Helsinki. September: one-man show (66 prints), University of Warsaw. October 17–December 16: in exhibition *Ideas in Images*, organized by Peter Pollack at Worcester Art Museum, Massachusetts.

1963

March: one-man exhibition, Galeria Krzysztofory, Krakow, Poland. April: one-man show, Carl Siembab Gallery, Boston. May 1: in exhibition *Contemporary Photographs from the Permanent Collection of The Art Institute of Chicago*. April 14–May 12: in exhibition *Ten Photographers*, Schuman Gallery, Rochester, New York. September 2–20: one-man exhibition, Galeria Towarzystwo, Warsaw. Wins 1963 Photographic Award at the Rhode Island Arts Festival. September 23–November 28: in exhibition *The Photographer and the American Landscape* (10 photographs), The Museum of Modern Art.

1964

Appointed professor, Rhode Island School of Design. March 2–April 4: one-man show, The Heliography Gallery, New York. September 1–November 12, 1966: in *Photography 64/An Invitational Exhibition*, co-sponsored by The New York State Exposition and George Eastman House; first shown at Exposition. May 27–May 5, 1965: in opening exhibition of The Edward Steichen Photography Center, The Museum of Modern Art. May 27–August 23: in *The Photographer's Eye*, The Museum of Modern Art. Summer: publication of *Photographs: Harry Callahan* (see bibl. 6). August 17–October 10: in honor of this monograph an exhibition of the same title was held at The Hall-mark Gallery, New York (and subsequently sent on tour) with an introduction by Edward Steichen: "If photographer Harry Callahan had chosen to work in any other medium, the art of photography would have lost one of its finest practitioners. In the brief history of the medium, he is one of the few whose work has contributed to lifting the mechanical proc-esses in the realm of the arts. . . . Photography and photographers have reason to be proud of Harry Cal-lahan and his work. Both as a photographer and as a person, he merits what was the top accolade in my boyhood days: 'He is all wool and a yard wide.'" Hallmark purchased the entire exhibition (150 prints) for its permanent collection.

1965
June 14: Having been invited by President Johnson to participate in The White House Festival of the Arts, he attended ceremonies in Washington, D.C.

1966
Late March–April 13: one-man exhibition at Reed College Kiosk Galleries, Portland, Oregon. May 20–July 31: in exhibition *Design for Living*, The Art In-stitute of Chicago. August 22–September 6: gave master class in photography under the auspices of the Letters and Science Extension of the University of California at Berkeley. Hallmark published a 1967 calendar, *Photographs by Harry Callahan*, reproducing 12 subjects.

1967
February 16–May, 1968: included in exhibition *Pho-tography in the Twentieth Century* prepared for The National Gallery of Canada by George Eastman House and circulated in Canada by the National Gal-lery. Sabbatical approved by the Rhode Island School of Design (plans to spend six months in Italy in 1968). The inscription in *Portfolio 67*, the Yearbook of the Rhode Island School of Design, reads:

"Harry Callahan
has dedicated himself
to photography, teaching and people.
We thank him.
This book is dedicated to
Harry Callahan."

Selected Bibliography by Bernard Karpel

Books and other General Works

1 Abbott, Berenice. *New Guide to Better Photography*. Rev. ed. New York: Crown Publishers, 1935, pp. 20, 52.

2 American Society of Magazine Photographers. *A.S.M.P. Picture Annual*. New York: Simon and Schuster, 1957, pp. 22–27 incl. 6 illus.
   Brief text by Callahan.

3 Barr, Alfred H., Jr., ed. *Masters of Modern Art*. New York: The Museum of Modern Art, 1954, p. 198 (illus.), bibl.
   In Edward Steichen's chapter on photography.

4 Callahan, Harry. *Motions*. Two-reel film, black-and-white, 16 mm., silent. Chicago, *ca.* 1949.
   Print, approximately 400 feet, in possession of Callahan. Shown publicly, for educational purposes only, at Pennsylvania State College (1951), and for lecture tour in Europe by Hugo Weber (Oslo, Zurich, Basel, 1952).

5 Callahan, Harry. *The Multiple Image: Photographs by Harry Callahan*. Chicago: Institute of Design of the Illinois Institute of Technology, 1961. 20 pp. incl. 18 illus. plus covers.
   Gordon Martin, Aaron Siskind, eds. Introduction by Jonathan Williams. Biographical note.

6 Callahan, Harry. *Photographs: Harry Callahan*. Santa Barbara: Van Riper & Thompson, 1964. 16 pp. plus 126 pl.
   Introduction by Hugo Weber. Captions and statements by Callahan. Extensive bibliography by Bernard Karpel, including exhibition catalogues.

7 Callahan, Harry. *1967: Photographs by Harry Callahan*. [New York?]: Hallmark Cards, [1966]. 12 pl.
   A calendar, with brief note by Edward Steichen (*see* page 79).

8 Callahan, Harry. "An Adventure in Photography," in Nathan Lyons, ed., *Photographers on Photography*. Englewood, N.J.: Prentice-Hall, 1966, pp. 40–41, 179 (bibl.).
   Autobiographical note, originally published in *Minicam Photography* (Cincinnati), no. 6, 1946, pp. 28–29.

9 Dorfles, Gillo. "Photography," in *Encyclopedia of World Art*. New York: McGraw-Hill Book Co., 1959, vol. 11, p. 31.

10 Downs, Bruce, ed. *Color Photography Annual 1956*. New York: Ziff-Davis, 1956, p. 90 (illus.).

11 Eigner, Larry. *On My Eyes*. Highland, N.C.: Jonathan Williams, 1960. [124] pp. incl. 12 illus. ("Jargon Press Edition," 36).
   Poems accompanied by Callahan's photographs.

12 *Funk & Wagnall's Standard Reference Encyclopedia: Year Book of Events of 1962*. New York: Funk & Wagnall: 1963, p. 259.

13 Knapp, Dee, Compiler. [Photographic work of Harry Callahan: a comprehensive pictorial record]. New York, 196?.
   A microfilm or similar photocopy of the total oeuvre, to be completed and deposited for research purposes in The Museum of Modern Art.

14 Knapp, Dee. "Callahan," in Willard D. Morgan, ed., *Encyclopedia of Photography*. New York:

Greystone, 1963, vol. 3, pp. 500–502 illus.

15 Lacey, Peter. *The History of the Nude in Photography*. New York: Bantam Books, 1964, pp. 86–97 incl. 7 illus. ("Bantam Gallery Edition").

16 Lyons, Nathan. *Photography in the Twentieth Century*. New York: Horizon Press, 1967, pp. viii, xi, 72 (illus.).
A picture book issued on the occasion of exhibition at the George Eastman House, Rochester (*see* page 79).

17 Newhall, Beaumont. *The History of Photography from 1839 to the Present Day*. Rev. ed. New York: The Museum of Modern Art, 1964, p. 200, 201 (illus.).
Fourth enlarged edition based on *Photography 1839–1937* (The Museum of Modern Art, 1937). Issued in collaboration with George Eastman House, Rochester.

18 Newhall, Beaumont. *Photography at Mid-Century*. Rochester, N.Y.: George Eastman House, 1959, p. 30.
Issued on the occasion of exhibition (*see* page 78).

19 *Photography Annual 1960. Compiled by the Editors of Popular Photography*. New York: Ziff-Davis, 1959, p. 115.
Also occasionally reproduced in the magazine proper, e.g., April 1961, p. 49.

20 *Photography of the World '66*. Tokyo: Heibonsha, 1966, pp. 17, 18 (port.) plus 6 pl.
English insert: notes on the pictures from *Photographs: Harry Callahan* (*see* bibl. 6).

21 Pollack, Peter J. *The Picture History of Photography*. New York: Harry N. Abrams, 1958, pp. 432–443 incl. 8 illus.
Revised edition in preparation.

22 *Portfolio 67*. Providence, R.I.: Rhode Island School of Design [1967] p. [2–3].
Frontispiece portrait, with student dedication to Callahan.

23 Steichen, Edward. *The Family of Man*. New York: Maco Magazine Corp., 1955, p. 190 (illus.).
(Published for The Museum of Modern Art). Issued in both clothbound and paperbound format on occasion of exhibition. Numerous reprintings (*see* page 78).
Steichen, Edward. See bibl. 3.

24 Steinert, Otto. *Subjektive Fotografie: 2*. Bonn: Auer, 1955, p. 27.
Exhibition catalogue (*see* page 78).

25 Szarkowski, John. *The Photographer and the American Landscape*. New York: The Museum of Modern Art, 1963, p. 47 (port.) plus 1 pl.
Exhibition catalogue (*see* page 78).

26 Szarkowski, John. *The Photographer's Eye*. New York: The Museum of Modern Art, 1966, pp. 107, 134 (2 illus.).
Book based on 1964 exhibition (*see* page 78).

27 U.S. Camera. *The Figure from U.S. Camera*. New York: U.S. Camera Publishing Corp., 1952, p. 92 (illus.).

28 Worcester Art Museum. *Ideas and Images*. Worcester, Mass.: The Museum, 1962, pp. 42–45, 49 plus 3 pl.
Exhibition catalogue. Essay and notes by Peter Pollack. Exhibition reviewed by E. Densmore

in *Worcester Sunday Telegram*, Oct. 7, 1962, pp. 12–15 illus.

29 Worth, Peter. "A Note on the Photographs of Callahan," in *University of Nebraska Galleries. No. 1: Four Gallery Talks*. Lincoln: University of Nebraska Press, 1952, pp. 65–72.
    Mimeographed. Important critique with literary references; mentions an aesthetic based on "the soundless explosions of memory."

Articles and Reviews

30 "The Artful Flow of Information," *Think* (New York), June 1960, pp. 18–21 incl. 6 illus.

31 "Best Photographs of 1963," *American Alumni Council News* (Washington, D.C.), June 1963, frontis.

32 Breitenbach, Joseph. "Look Here, Diogenes!" *Infinity* (New York), May 1952. pp. 7, 14 (illus.).
    Refers to exhibition at The Museum of Modern Art (*see* page 79).

33 Callahan, Harry. [Photo: *La terrasse nord de l'Harmes*], *L'Arc* (Aix-en-Provence), no. 2, 1958, p. 71.
    Representative of work during European trip publicized in a number of journals (*see* page 79).

34 Callahan, Harry. [Ten photographs], *Gentry* (New York), Fall 1956, pp. 41–49 (all illus.).

35 [Callahan clipping file]. New York, Museum of Modern Art Department of Photography, various dates.
    Miscellaneous materials including catalogues, checklists, artists' records, and notes. Typescripts: statement by Callahan "about 1952," statement by Steichen "about 1952"; publicity releases, captions, etc.

36 "Camera clinic: Do You See What You Look at?" *Chicago Daily News Magazine*, May 19, 1951, 4 illus.
    Photographs from current show at the Art Institute (*see* page 78).

37 "Chicago Highlights Photography," *Pictures on Exhibit* (New York), May 1951, pp. 6–7 illus.
    Refers to exhibition at the Art Institute. Similarly *This Week in Chicago*, May 19, 1951: "Creative Photography Show" (*see* page 76).

38 Coke, Van Deren. "An Exhibition: 'Creative Photography–1956,' " *Aperture* (Rochester), no. 1, 1956, p. 22 illus.
    Refers to Exhibition at George Eastman House (*see* page 77).

39 Creeley, Robert. "Harry Callahan: A Note," *Black Mountain Review* (N.C.), Autumn 1957, p. 149–150 plus 8 illus.

40 Czartoryska, Urszula. "Harry Callahan in Polsce," *Fotografia* (Warsaw), Mar. 1963, pp. 71–74 incl. 6 illus.
    Resumés in Russian, German, French, and English.

41 "Diogenes with a Camera," *New York Times Magazine*, June 1, 1952, pp. 42–43 (illus.).

42 Dunn, Jack. "35mm. Clairvoyance," *Chicago*, Nov. 1955, pp. 39–41 illus.
    Photographs by Callahan with captions by Dunn.

43 Ebin, David. "Harry Callahan: Conventional Subjects Become Extraordinary Photographs," *Modern Photography* (New York), Feb. 1957, pp. 45–55, 98, 102, 106 incl. 18 illus. (1 color).

Quotes letter by Callahan (Jan. 30, 1946; *see* page 6) to The Museum of Modern Art, his personal statement of 1946 (*see* bibl. 8), and other citations.

44 "Façades by Harry Callahan," *Chicago*, Apr. 1955, pp. 3–5 incl. 8 illus.

45 "Four photographers," *U.S. Camera* (New York), Feb. 1949, pp. 36–37 illus.

On exhibition at the The Museum of Modern Art.

46 "Harry Callahan: Folio 1," *Choice* (Chicago), no. 2, 1962, 9 illus. following p. 49.

47 Jouffroy, Alain. "La XXVIIIᵉ biennale de Venise," *Arts* (Paris), no. 573, 1956, p. 14.

Comments on *American Artists Paint the City* exhibition, praising the one item not in the official catalogues: a large photomontage by Callahan (*see* page 77).

48 Karr, S. P. "The Third Eye," *Art Photography* (Chicago), Sept. 1952, pp. 34–36 illus.

On the photography department at the Institue of Design.

49 Munroe, Joe. "Harry Callahan," *Infinity* (New York), Jan. 1965, pp. 16–23 incl. 7 illus.

50 "Museum's Great Photographs," *Coronet Magazine* (Chicago), Nov. 1960, pp. 136–137 incl. 1 illus.

On the collection of The Museum of Modern Art.

51 "One in a Thousand," *Newsweek* (Dayton, Ohio), May 7, 1951, p. 4–8 illus.

Review of Callahan show at The Chicago Art Institute.

52 Rotzler, Willy. "Harry M. Callahan: 7 Farbaufnahmen," *Du* (Zurich), Jan. 1962, pp. 38–46 incl. 7 color pl., 1 port.

53 Sandburg, Carl. "Carl Sandburg and His Chicago," *Chicago Sunday Tribune Magazine*, Mar. 10, 1957, pp. 6–9 illus.

Extracts from poems; photographs by Callahan.

54 Steichen, Edward. "The New Selective Lens," *Art News* (New York), Sept. 1950, pp. 22–25, 1 illus.

55 ———. "Photographer's Choice," *New York Times Magazine*, Mar. 28, 1954, pp. 26–27 incl. 1 illus.

56 ———. "Photography at the Museum of Modern Art," *Bulletin of the Museum of Modern Art*, no. 4, 1952, p. [16] (illus.).

Special number on work of the department. Additional illustration, no. 4, 1948, p. 15.

57 "Visions of beauty," *Camera* (Lucerne), Apr. 1959, pp. 26–27 illus.

58 Weiss, Margaret R. "Double exposure," *Saturday Review* (New York), Sept. 26, 1967, pp. 36–38 incl. 7 illus. (port.).

On the occasion of exhibition at the Hallmark Gallery.

59 Weiss, Margaret R. "Ideas in images," *Saturday Review* (New York), Dec. 29, 1962, pp. 20–23 incl. 1 illus.

Review of American Federation of Arts show (*see* page 78).

60 White, Minor. "The Photographs of Harry Callahan," *Aperture* (Rochester), no. 2, 1958, pp. 70–73 incl. 3 illus.
    Review of exhibition at George Eastman House.

61 White, Minor, ed. "The Sense of Abstraction in Contemporary Photography," *Aperture* (Roch-ester), no. 2, 1960, p. 116 (illus.).
    Special issue based on Museum of Modern Art exhibition (*see* page 78). Brief texts by White and Nathan Lyons.

62 White, Minor, ed. "The Way through Camera Work," *Aperture* (Rochester), no. 2, 1959, p. 59 (illus.).
    Confronting text titled "a psychological ex-planation of contemplation."